EVERYTHING YOU KNOW ABOUT MINIBEASTS IS WRONG!

DR. NICK CRUMPTON
and GAVIN SCOTT

nosy crow

FOR ELLA
N. C.

**FOR MY AMAZING NIECE VIOLET,
WITH LOVE**
G. S.

First published 2022 by Nosy Crow Ltd
The Crow's Nest, 14 Baden Place,
Crosby Row, London, SE1 1YW, UK

Nosy Crow Eireann Limited
44 Orchard Grove, Kenmare,
Co Kerry, V93 FY22, Ireland

www.nosycrow.com

ISBN 978 1 83994 203 7

Nosy Crow and associated logos are trademarks
and/or registered trademarks of Nosy Crow Ltd.

Text © Nick Crumpton 2022
Illustrations © Gavin Scott 2022

With special thanks to Ross Piper for his expert advice and extra thanks
to Lewis Bartlett, Gavin Broad, Beulah Garner and Stephen Montgomery.

The right of Nick Crumpton to be identified as the author and Gavin Scott
to be identified as the illustrator of this work has been asserted.

A CIP catalogue record for this book is available from the British Library.

Printed in China.
Papers used by Nosy Crow are made from wood
grown in sustainable forests.

1 3 5 7 9 8 6 4 2

CONTENTS

INTRODUCTION

During the 4.5-billion-year history of life on earth, certain sorts of animals have done *EXTREMELY* well at different times.

The Devonian period (419–359 million years ago), for example, was the 'Age of the Fish', while the Mesozoic era (252–66 million years ago) was the 'Age of the Dinosaurs'. Most people will tell you that we are now living in the 'Age of the Mammals', but, really, for the last 400 million years, the Earth has belonged to one astonishing group of animals – the *INSECTS*!

Just take a look at some of these numbers . . .

Two thirds of *all* the species of animals that scientists have discovered and described on Earth are insects.

This means that if you chose one species completely at random, from the enormous messy web of life, from among whales, tigers, lizards, sharks, jellyfish, squids, frogs and birds . . . two out of every three times, you'd pick a bee, a wasp, a fly or an earwig!

There are more than 200 MILLION INSECTS FOR EVERY SINGLE HUMAN BEING living on Planet Earth today! And they are everywhere – living in fresh water, in the air, under the ground, and in the ocean.

In fact, insects are actually just one type of animal that belong to a larger group of animals called arthropods and, all together, it's thought that the 8 billion humans on this planet live alongside 10 QUINTILLION crabs, bees, copepods, flies, gnats, centipedes and all the other amazing animals you will meet in this book. Of all the creatures humans have discovered and named, eight out of ten of them are arthropods. So that means if you chose another species at random from the big messy web, eight times out of ten, you'd pick an arthropod!

Together with other animals without backbones, like slugs, snails and worms, these minibeasts show a massive amount of DIVERSITY – or differences between each other. This means that even if you know some amazing facts about some minibeasts, it's impossible to know everything about all of them. And lots of the things you might know about some minibeasts are actually completely WRONG for others.

(And you might not know the minibeasts you think you know very well at all . . .)

So, let's jump into the undergrowth and find out just how wrong everything you know about minibeasts really is!

ALL MINIBEASTS ARE INSECTS . . . AND ALL INSECTS ARE BUGS

WRONG!

When it comes to the words we use to talk about bees, beetles and butterflies, things are a *bit* more confusing than they might seem at first . . . For instance, lots of people talk about minibeasts as though they're all insects . . . but they're *not*. And 'bugs' are only a special, particular *sort* of insect.

Spiders *definitely* aren't insects, and snails are more closely related to octopuses than any of the other animals on this page! Confused? Don't be! Just take a look at this handy guide to who's who.

In this book (and whenever you're outside) you're going to meet a lot of *ARTHROPODS*. This isn't a very common word, but you already know what arthropods are. They are animals without backbones that have jointed legs and a strong outer-casing called an exoskeleton which is split into lots of segments. This helps to protect them and holds all their insides in place.

There are **FOUR** main types of arthropods: the *INSECTS*, the *MYRIAPODS*, the *ARACHNIDS*, and the *CRUSTACEANS*.

INSECTS are arthropods that have six legs and three main body parts – the head, thorax and abdomen. Beetles, wasps, butterflies, moths, flies and bugs* are the most common types of insects on Earth.

*True 'bugs' are actually insects from just one group, called the Hemiptera. They all have sucking mouthparts that most use to slurp sap out of plants . . . so next time someone says a beetle is a bug . . . tell them to watch their mouth (and the bug's)!

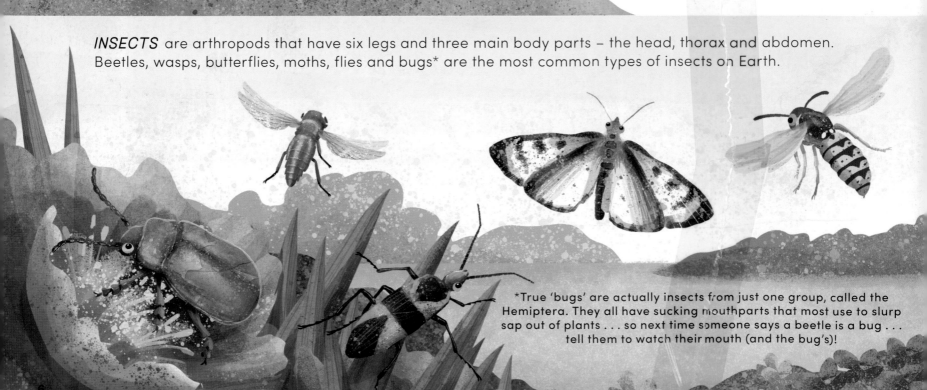

MYRIAPODS, such as centipedes and millipedes, have a hard exoskeleton, like insects. But they all have *more* than six legs. In some cases many, *many* more.

Spiders and harvestmen (along with a few other oddballs you'll meet later in this book) are *ARACHNIDS*. They have more than six legs, but only two main body sections.

Lastly, **CRUSTACEANS** are to the sea what insects are to the land. These exoskeleton-clad water-wonders include animals like shrimp and lobsters and stranger creatures like barnacles.

As well as these segmented animals, there are a few other minibeasts that you'll meet in this book, like slugs and snails and many types of worms, that aren't arthropods at all. They just happen to be mini. Slugs and snails are *GASTROPODS* and . . . well, you'll find out about worms later!

So now you know what are – and what AREN'T – bugs and insects, let's take a closer look at some other 'facts' that might need a bit of sorting out.

INSECTS ARE AS OLD AS THE DINOSAURS

WRONG!

Excellent knowledge! By the time the first dinosaurs evolved in the Triassic period they were sharing the world with buzzing, swarming, crawling, nibbling insects. But here's the thing . . . insects are EVEN OLDER than the very first dinosaurs – and by quite a long way!

The very first insects, such as *RHYNIOGNATHA*, looked similar to mayflies today and evolved from other arthropods almost *500 million years ago*, which means insects have been around for more than TWICE as long as dinosaurs! The world for early insects was warm, early forests were beginning to grow and the Earth's first land predators – small arachnids and ancient centipedes – were starting to stalk the ground.

Meganeura

Arthropleura

Meganeura

CARBONIFEROUS PERIOD

359–300 MILLION YEARS AGO

Insect fossils are incredibly rare to find, and even more so from the ancient time when they first appeared, but we know more about the early insects from the *CARBONIFEROUS* period, about 359 to 300 million years ago. This wet, warm, green world was a paradise for early arthropods, which, thanks to very high oxygen levels, grew to astonishing sizes.

Huge relatives of today's millipedes, such as *ARTHROPLEURA*, wandered over forest floors alongside relatives of cockroaches and grasshoppers. The first flying insects also evolved, such as *MEGANEURA*, a relative of dragonflies that flew on wings reaching 70 centimetres across, the same as that of a kestrel today.

Insects can be fossilised into rocks, but the chances of this happening are pretty small. Some of the most spectacular fossils of insects have instead been found in amber (a fossilised liquid that seeped out of some trees millions of years ago), which some people like to wear as fancy jewellery. These don't just preserve impressions of insects but whole animals trapped in time! An ant being attacked by a parasite, a wasp being captured by a spider, even a 100-million-year-old shield bug carrying its eggs have all been spotted by scientists in these orangey gems.

With every year that passes, more and more ancient insects are discovered in amber, so scientists keep learning about the deep history of this terrifically huge – and terrifically old – group of animals.

PERMIAN PERIOD
300–252 MILLION YEARS AGO

MESOZOIC ERA
252–66 MILLION YEARS AGO

SNAKEFLIES and *BEETLES* evolved during the Permian period while the world's continents were all colliding together, forming the supercontinent Pangea.

There was a mass extinction event caused by catastrophic volcanic activity at the end of the Permian period, but insects weren't too badly affected and the first *WASPS*, *TRUE BUGS*, *CRANE FLIES*, and *THRIPS* all began to evolve while the first dinosaurs began roaming the Earth.

At the beginning of the Mesozoic era insects continued to diversify, and the relationship between flowers and insects began at least 99 million years ago, by which time the pollinating beetle *ANGIMORDELLA BURMITINA* was sharing pollen between plants – and so were some of the first bees.

BEES DIE WHEN THEY STING YOU

WRONG!

Bees (which are actually vegetarian wasps!) have been buzzing around the world for at least 100 million years – and we all know something pretty unfortunate that happens to them when they sting people . . .

Western honey bee

The tip of their stings are serrated, like the backwards-facing teeth of a saw. Although this means their stings can dig into the flesh of an enemy to help pump in a dose of painful venom, the backwards-barbs catch in their target's skin. As the bee tries to fly away the stinger can't be pulled out and it has to tear its body away from its embedded weapon which, sadly, causes the bee to die . . .

Apis honeybee

Well . . . Actually it is *only* the stingers of the seven species of *APIS HONEYBEES* that are serrated like this – and even then, it's only the females (those that aren't the queen)! Considering that there are over 20,000 species of bees in the world, this means that pretty much all bees with stingers don't worry about flying away with parts of their bodies missing!

Apis honeybees, like the **WESTERN HONEY BEE**, are able to sting other insects and not lose their stings. It's just that the skin of mammals is much tougher and bees cannot slide the stinger out as easily as they could from a smaller enemy.

6 cm

2 mm

Perdita minima

Wallace's giant bee

Honeybees are what most people think of when they think about bees. But, from the tiny *PERDITA MINIMA* to the gigantic *WALLACE'S GIANT BEE*, the world of bees is much more *diverse* than you might think.

Some, like *TETRAGONISCA ANGUSTULA* from South America and the *SUGARBAG BEE* of Australia don't have stings at all and some, like the *VULTURE BEE*, don't feed on pollen and nectar but eat up the remains of dead animals in a similar way to maggots.

Orchid bee

Tetragonisca angustula

Lots of bees, such as the *ORCHID BEE*, aren't yellow and black either, and most species of orchid bees don't have queens!

Blue carpenter bee

Mason bee

Vulture bee

Tawny mining bee

We might think all bees live in hives but more than 90% of bees live by themselves or in small groups. Mining bees like the *TAWNY MINING BEE* build underground tunnels to live and grow in, carpenter bees like the *BLUE CARPENTER BEE* dig tunnels into dead wood, and *MASON BEES* use these nests and tunnels after they have been abandoned.

Black and yellow coats, making honey, even death by stinging . . . bees are a great example of how many of the things you might have been told define a type of insect aren't necessarily true for all the species in a group.

13

CENTIPEDES HAVE 100 LEGS

WRONG!

Lots of languages have similar names for centipedes: in Spanish, they are *ciempiés*; if you speak Afrikaans, you might know them as *honderdpoot*, and the Germans call them *hundertfüßer*. These all mean 'hundred feet', but do they really have 100?

The answer is . . . it depends on the species! But one thing is for certain: no centipede in the world has 100 legs.

This is because the number of pairs of legs centipedes have is always odd and, as 100 legs would need 50 pairs, this just doesn't add up. Species could only have either 98 legs (with 49 pairs of legs), or 102 (with 51).

Aside from this, all 3,000 species of centipede – from the common *EUROPEAN BROWN CENTIPEDE* to the *FLORIDA BLUE CENTIPEDE* – have certain things in common.

They are fast-moving predators, are all relatively soft in comparison to some arthropods, and they all prey on the animals they hunt with a pair of poisoned leg-like claws near their head called forcipules.

European brown centipede

Florida blue centipede

The centipede with the most number of legs is the soil centipede *HIMANTARIUM GABRIELIS*, which can have over 342 legs!

Himantarium gabrielis

But what about millipedes? Well, as you might have guessed, none of the 12,000 known species of millipede have 1,000 legs.

Millipedes, like the **AMERICAN GIANT MILLIPEDE**, are hard-bodied, slow-moving vegetarians that have TWO pairs of legs on each segment. Many of them protect themselves by releasing toxic chemicals at would-be predators – like the *CYANIDE MILLIPEDE*.

Millipedes generally have around 300 legs, but one species is known to have more than 1,000! In 2020, *EUMILLIPES PERSEPHONE* was discovered 60 metres underground and it has the most legs of any animal known on Earth – up to a humongous 1,306 – even though their bodies are only about 10 centimetres long!

Lots of other millipedes, such as the woodlouse-like *PILL MILLIPEDE*, are stubby and only have 17 to 19 pairs of legs.

American giant millipede

Illacme plenipes

Cyanide millipede

Pill millipede

Animal names can be tricky. After all, the 'cent' in 'centipede' means 100 (a century is 100 years, a centimetre is 100th of a metre), and the 'mill' in 'millipede' comes from the Latin (and French) for a thousand. If you want to use the most correct words for these animals . . . stick to their scientific names! Instead of 'centipedes', use Chilopoda, which means 'lip-legs' (their forcipules!), and instead of 'millipedes', use Diplopoda, which means 'double-foot' – the two pairs of legs per section.

FLIES ALL LOOK THE SAME

WRONG!

All flies have heads they can easily move around, large eyes and a shrunken rear pair of wings that have changed into stabilisers for helping them fly like daredevils, but aside from this there is an amazing amount of DIVERSITY between the different sorts of flies . . . They're not all small, round or annoying!

MOSQUITOES are famous for sucking blood. But only the females actually do it, and even then only some of the time. They pierce animals' skin with a set of needle-like sharp mouthparts.

Mosquito

Not very many flies have long antennae like those found on mosquitoes, apart from the furry 'moth' flies like the BATHROOM MOTH MIDGE.

Bathroom moth midge

Robber fly

ROBBER FLIES are powerful killers that catch their prey mid-flight.

Horsefly

HORSEFLIES are blood-feeders that grow up in mud and water. Although they are called 'horse' flies, different species prefer different prey . . . such as Tabanus bigutatus, otherwise called the HIPPO FLY.

BEE FLIES look incredibly similar to bees and live very similar lives, feeding on nectar and pollen.

Bee fly

LONG-LEGGED FLIES, like TELOSTYLINUS LINEOLATUS are slender flies that eat rotting plants and vegetables.

Long-legged fly

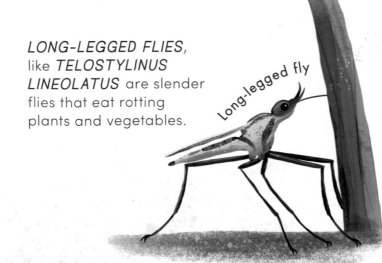

Mydas fly

The MYDAS FLIES, like GAUROMYDAS HEROS, are among the largest flies in the world – reaching lengths of up to 7 centimetres.

HOVERFLIES are some of the most skilled flyers in the animal kingdom.

Hoverfly

The **PHORID FLIES** are one of the smallest animals in the world, including *Euryplatea nanaknihali*, which is less than half a millimetre long!

Phorid fly

The **KEDS** are a group of flies, many of which have lost their wings and look and act like lice.

Keds

The **RICHARDIIDAE** are a group of flies with beautiful wings from the tropics of Central America.

Richardiidae

MARSH FLIES are long-legged flies that tend to live near ponds and rivers.

Marsh fly

The mysterious, almost spherical **BEETLE FLIES** hide their wings under a shell. Biologists don't know an awful lot about these peculiar flies.

Beetle fly

The eyes of the **STALK-EYED FLIES** sit on the end of long stalks that adults pump outwards when they emerge from their pupae.

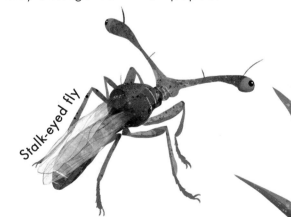
Stalk-eyed fly

Although most of us think flies are just bluebottles, house flies and (maybe, if you're smart) hoverflies, there are over 130,000 known species . . . and there may be thousands more than this! Because the insect world is so bewilderingly full of different species it's tricky to describe what 'a' fly looks like. Or 'a' bee, or 'a' beetle. Instead, when it comes to insects it's best to think that if you can imagine it, there's probably a species that looks like it!

INSECTS ARE UGLY

Most humans don't see much beauty when they see an insect. But insects don't try to look pretty for humans. They look the way they do either to better survive in their environment or to attract mates of their own species.

But out of the unbelievably huge number of insects out there, there are some that are pretty amazing-looking even to human eyes . . .

GREEN MILKWEED GRASSHOPPER

GREEN MILKWEED GRASSHOPPERS (*Phymateus viridipes*) are actually large locusts from Africa that have red and blue hindwings.

ASIAN LANTERNFLY

The long-faced *ASIAN LANTERNFLY* (*Pyrops candelaria*) is a planthopper bug that sucks sap from trees in Southeast Asia.

PICASSO MOTH

Baorisa hieroglyphica is sometimes called the *PICASSO MOTH*, after the Spanish painter Pablo Picasso, whose painting looked similar to the patterns on its wings.

BLUE-GREEN WEEVIL

The *BLUE-GREEN WEEVIL* (*Eupholus schoenherri*) lives in the forests of New Guinea.

PANDA ANT

The *PANDA ANT* (*Euspinolia militaris*) is actually a wingless wasp from Chile.

BRUSH JEWEL BEETLE

The blue wing case of the *BRUSH JEWEL BEETLE* (*Julodis cirrosa*) is punctured all over with orange hairs.

FLOWER CHAFER

The *FLOWER CHAFER* (*Argyripa gloriosa*) is a particularly beautiful large beetle related to dung beetles.

PANCHLORA KOZANEKI

PANCHLORA KOZANEKI is a particularly beautiful cockroach from the Amazon forests of Peru.

RUBY-TAILED CUCKOO WASP

The *RUBY-TAILED CUCKOO WASP* (*Chrysis ruddii*) is a solitary wasp that can curl itself into a protective ball.

EMERALD COCKROACH WASP

EMERALD COCKROACH WASPS (*Ampulex compressa*) are beautiful, but inject venom into their prey's brains to turn them into controllable zombies!

JEWEL SCARAB BEETLE

Light is reflected off the *JEWEL SCARAB BEETLE* (*Chrysina resplendens*) so it looks like it's made from gold.

IMPERIAL ARCAS

The *IMPERIAL ARCAS* (*Arcas imperialis*) is a stunning butterfly from Colombia.

PINK FLOWER MANTIS

The *PINK FLOWER MANTIS* (*Hymenopus coronatus*) disguises itself as an orchid in order to strike at unsuspecting prey visiting the flower for nectar.

LUNA MOTH

The long wing tails of the *LUNA MOTH* (*Actias luna*) confuse the sonar of the bats that hunt them and help them escape being caught mid-flight.

ONCOMETOPIA ORBONA

ONCOMETOPIA ORBONA is a spectacularly coloured sharpshooter bug from North America. After drinking sap, they 'sharpshoot' what they don't digest out of their rear ends!

WHITE NAMIB DARKLING BEETLE

The *WHITE NAMIB DARKLING BEETLE* (*Onymacris candidipennis*) is bright white – but this is caused by light reflecting off them, rather than their actual colour.

ROSY MAPLE MOTH

The *ROSY MAPLE MOTH* (*Dryocampa rubicunda*) lives in North America and spends most of its time around maple trees.

GREEN BOTTLE FLY

The common *GREEN BOTTLE FLY* (*Lucilia sericata*) is a fly known for feeding on dead things, but its red eyes and brilliant bright green and blue exoskeleton make it striking up close.

Seeing these extraordinary animals together makes it easier to understand why some insects have been considered beautiful for thousands of years. So, next time you have the chance to *really* look at a bee or a dragonfly, take as close a look as you possibly can and see if you can see some beauty . . .

HONEYBEES ARE THE MOST IMPORTANT POLLINATORS

WRONG!

Pollination is the movement of grains of pollen from male plant parts to female plant parts in order to create seeds, out of which new, young plants can grow – but lots of plants need a helping hand. Somewhere in the region of 80% of *all* plants on Earth rely on insects moving pollen between flowers in order to create a new generation of plants.

It's true that honeybees are extremely important pollinators. They transfer pollen between flowers as it gets stuck on their furry bodies when they eat nectar, but the solitary mason bees, like the *BLUE ORCHARD MASON BEE*, are actually some of the best bees at pollinating plants.

MASON BEES are more active at chillier temperatures than honeybees, so they can help plants pollinate earlier in the year. They also each visit more flowers on average than individual bees from hives, *and* they are very messy and accidentally shower pollen on flowers as they fly over them.

Blue orchard mason bee

Blister beetle

HONEYBEES appeared more than 35 million years ago, but other insects were pollinating plants with flowers by some point in the Mesozoic era, and non-flowering plants even before that – and they still do today . . .

Thick-legged flower beetle

MOTHS help flowers rarely visited by other insects to pollinate during the night by carrying pollen on the hairs on their backs and on their wings.

WASPS also work as pollinators, and some are *extremely* picky when it comes to which plants they work with. Fig wasps pollinate the tiny flowers found *inside* the fruits of fig trees by laying their eggs within the fruit. The males live their entire lives inside the fruit, but the females escape and travel to another fig – taking pollen with them!

Fig wasp

HOVERFLIES are amazing pollinators. So are **MOSQUITOES**, which pollinate orchids. Other flies pollinate far less attractive species of flower – like the **BLOW FLIES** that pollinate the Indonesian rafflesia flower. It attracts pollinators by stinking of rotting flesh.

A huge range of beetles, including **BLISTER BEETLES**, **LONG-HORN BEETLES** and the **THICK-LEGGED FLOWER BEETLE**, transport pollen as they scuttle between flowering plants.

So it's not just honeybees that help flowers survive. Ecosystems – the webs of relationships between plants and animals in a habitat – are extremely complicated, and humans often don't see the connections between different living things. It's important we try to protect as many animals and plants as possible, because it's difficult to know all the important roles they play in the survival of other species.

Blow *fly*

Long-horn beetle

21

WE KNOW HOW MANY INSECTS THERE ARE

Remember those incredible numbers of insects we started this book with?
Two thirds of all known species, 200 million insects for every person . . .
That sure does sound impressive. But when it comes to *really* knowing how many
types of insects there are on Earth, the *truth* is that all these numbers are made up!
WAIT! COME BACK! You can still trust this book! You see, those numbers haven't
been made up out of *thin air* . . . but they are estimates.

The trouble is that trying to work out how many species
of insects and other minibeasts there are in the world
is incredibly difficult because people could never, ever
count them in all the different places that they live.

Even counting the number of species that live in one single
forest would be impossible. Instead, scientists who study insects
(called entomologists) 'sample' little areas. This means that they
count the number of species in one smaller place – like a single tree.
By beating or fogging a tree with a gas (to knock insects out of the
tree), entomologists can take the number of different minibeasts they
find and then, using very complicated maths, work out how many
species there would *probably* be in the whole forest.

What we *can* be sure about is that the number of types of insects we humans definitely know about increases by *hundreds* of species every year as they are discovered by entomologists. We also know that about 80% of the species of insects we know about live in the tropics, so that's where lots of scientists go to find them.

But insects are found almost everywhere. You don't have to jump on a boat to Brazil or a steamer to Sulawesi to look for new bees or beetles.

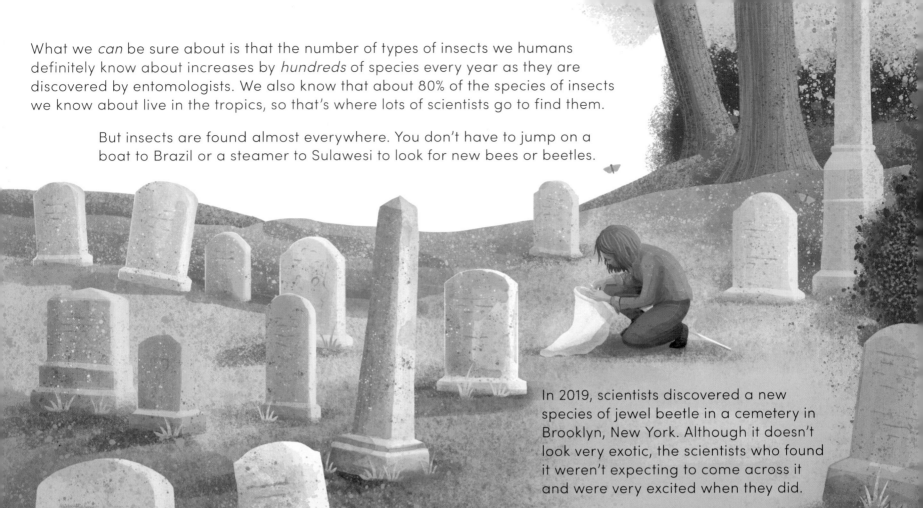

In 2019, scientists discovered a new species of jewel beetle in a cemetery in Brooklyn, New York. Although it doesn't look very exotic, the scientists who found it weren't expecting to come across it and were very excited when they did.

On the other side of the USA, scientists in Los Angeles were sure that if they set up insect traps around the city they would discover species no one had seen before . . . and they found lots, including 30 species of a single kind of Megaselia fly! They discovered even more when they were stuck at home during the coronavirus pandemic in 2020 and had lots of time on their hands.

MINI FACT!

Each new species discovered needs a name and scientists often honour their colleagues, friends, families – or heroes – by naming the newly discovered animals after them. In 2019, a species of beetle was named after the environmental campaigner Greta Thunberg and, in 2021, a rather beautiful soldier fly was named *Opaluma rupaul* after the equally sensational drag queen RuPaul.

Scientists think that there are probably more than twice the number of insects in the world than those that we know about, so there must be millions still to be discovered AT LEAST! So who knows . . . maybe you'll discover a new species in your local park. Or in your kitchen . . . or your bed?

YOU SOMETIMES EAT SPIDERS IN YOUR SLEEP

WRONG!

It's hard to know where exactly this 'fact' came from, but it is absolutely, completely, *definitely* not true.

Spiders don't have any reason for coming near your bed. They mostly spend their time waiting very patiently to trap prey, so they hang around in places like the corners of bathrooms or near windows, where the insects they like to feed on, like flies, moths and mosquitoes, will turn up.

If a spider *did* accidentally find itself near your mouth, it would be an awful place to camp out, and that's because of how spiders sense their environment.

Their most important sense is touch and with sensitive 'trichobothria' on their legs – just like dogs' or cats' whiskers – they feel the air for the buzzing vibrations of a pair of wings nearby.

So being anywhere near a person's mouth, with gusts of breath rushing in and out 20 times a minute, and the bed vibrating with snores, snorts and the occasional burp, would be a very confusing – and terrifying – place for a spider.

This isn't to say that some humans don't eat other minibeasts *on purpose* . . .

Around a quarter of all humans have enjoyed insects as part of their diet for thousands of years. It just doesn't seem to be very popular in Europe and North America.

Larvae of the *MEALWORM BEETLE* are sprinkled into lots of dishes in many countries in Southeast Asia, a bit like savoury hundreds-and-thousands; salty 'fat-bottomed' *LEAFCUTTER ANTS* are a popcorn-like delicacy in Colombia; and *CHAPULINE GRASSHOPPERS* are cooked and crunched inside tortillas in Mexico.

Eating *sustainably* farmed insects is a much more environmentally friendly way to get protein into our bodies. Unlike traditional farm animals, insects don't need lots of land to graze on, or much water to drink, and they produce hardly any global warming gases. Amazingly, a burger made from crickets has about the same amount of protein and calcium as one made from beef, but with much less fat.

So although you might not eat spiders in your sleep, you could start eating insects when you are awake! And that spider 'fact' goes to show that you shouldn't believe everything you read on the internet – or even what some grown-ups tell you (especially the ones who are afraid of spiders!).

ALL BEETLES EAT OTHER ANIMALS

WRONG!

Some beetles, like the common *LADYBIRD BEETLES* and many *GROUND BEETLES* are carnivorous. They're gardeners' friends, hunting and munching pests like greenflies that can kill plants, while in the water all *DIVING BEETLES* live carnivorous lives too.

These species have chewing and biting mouthparts, just like all other beetles. And there are a lot of other beetles. A LOT. There are more species of beetles on Earth than there are types of plants and – amazingly – almost one third of all known animals are beetles!

And not all beetles hunt garden pests . . . not even all ladybird beetles. The *MEXICAN LADYBIRD BEETLE* is completely vegetarian.

The truth is that most of the 380,000 species of beetles are strictly vegetarian when they are adults.

Rhinoceros beetle

Florida tortoise beetle

Some, like the *RHINOCEROS BEETLE*, eat so much that they are considered pests by farmers of coconut palms.

All 40,000 species of leaf beetles are herbivorous – like the *FLORIDA TORTOISE BEETLE* that oozes sticky oil from its feet so it can cling on to plant stems better while nibbling, or the *FROG-LEGGED LEAF BEETLE* that uses its enormous legs to stay wrapped round the plants they are eating.

Frog-legged leaf beetle

Oak splendour beetle

Some beetles have slightly different vegetarian diets.

Jewel beetles, like the **OAK SPLENDOUR BEETLE**, burrow into trees and their larvae eat the living tree's wood, which can cause big problems in forests.

Furniture beetle

Others, like the larvae of the **FURNITURE BEETLE**, are often called woodworm and can gnaw into wooden tables and chairs, making them brittle and fragile.

Ladybird

Some of the most spectacular vegetarian beetles are weevils. There are over ten times as many species of weevils than there are mammals and almost all are herbivorous.

Giraffe-necked weevil

Lots have long extended mouthparts – like the **CHESTNUT WEEVIL**.

Chestnut weevil

Other weevils may have shorter mouthparts but hugely extended 'neck' regions – like the **GIRAFFE-NECKED WEEVIL** from Madagascar.

Animals can be *very* picky when it comes to what they eat. And the pickier they are, the more different species there are, with each type of creature specialising in particular foods to munch. Vegetarian beetles found that the world was full of delicious plants they could snack on, and without this incredible diversity there would not be so many species of beetles clambering over them in search of their lunch today.

SLUGS AND SNAILS ONLY EAT LETTUCES

Gastropods (which means 'stomach foot'), like slugs and snails, are some of the easiest minibeasts to spot – and some of the most famous garden-destroying vegetarians. But rather than using their slicing mouthpart (called the radula) to scrape tasty morsels off plants, some slugs and snails are *carnivorous* and they eat their prey whole or slowly, slicing thin sections off piece by piece!

Gray-foot lancetooth

The Canadian *GRAY-FOOT LANCETOOTH* follows the slime trails of other snails, such as young, soft-shelled *FLAMED DISCS*, flipping them over before devouring them with its sharp-toothed radula.

The New Zealand native *AMBER SNAILS* dine on other minibeasts . . . like slugs.

Predatory glass snail

Amber snail

Carnivorous gastropods can sometimes look confusing as some slugs have shells, and some snails have only small ones! *PREDATORY GLASS SNAILS* have shells too small to hide in, while *WORM-EATING SLUGS* have a tiny shell at their rear end.

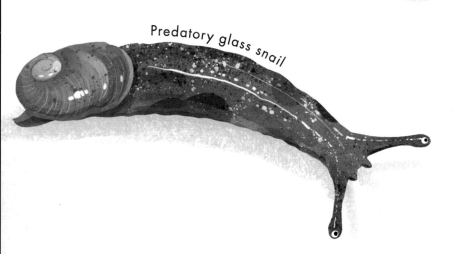

Worm-eating slug

Ghost slug

The white *GHOST SLUG* was discovered in Wales in 2008. It is blind, lives almost entirely under the ground and hunts earthworms at night.

The **TWO-TONED GULELLA** is a thin, small, carnivorous snail that originally lived in Asia or southern Africa but now lives (and hunts) all around the world. Humans accidentally spread them as stowaways on boats and planes over land.

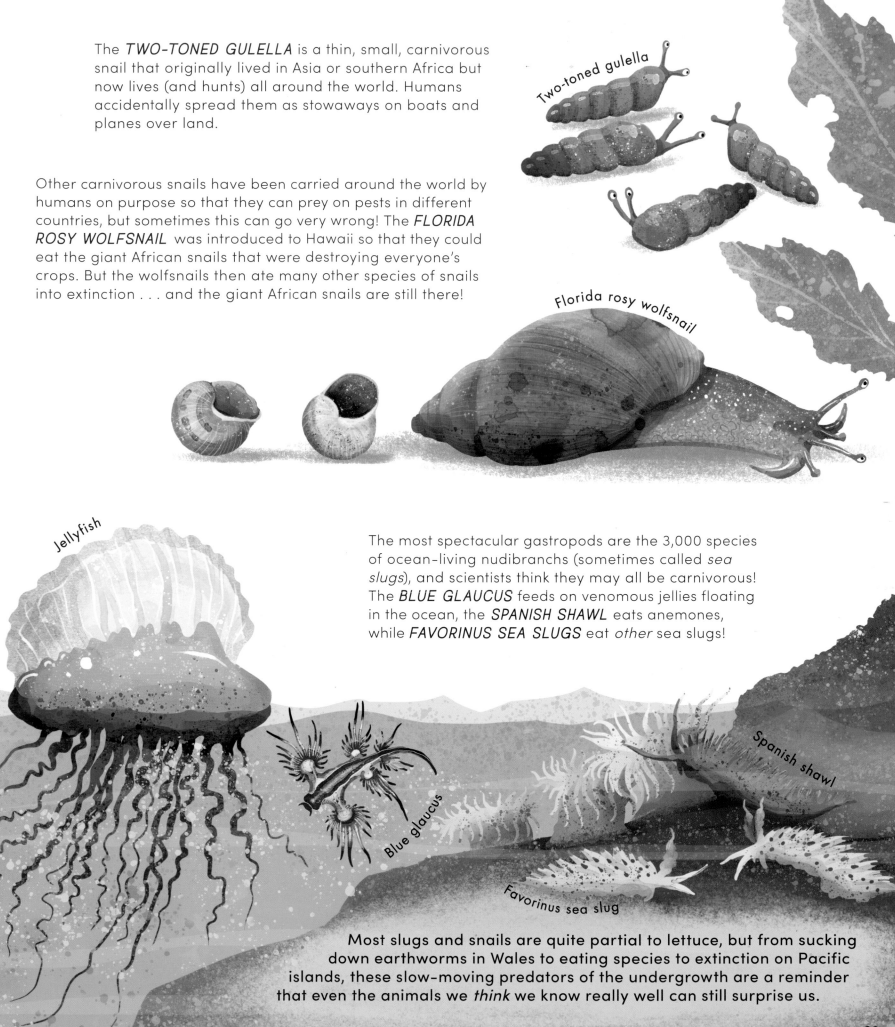

Two-toned gulella

Other carnivorous snails have been carried around the world by humans on purpose so that they can prey on pests in different countries, but sometimes this can go very wrong! The **FLORIDA ROSY WOLFSNAIL** was introduced to Hawaii so that they could eat the giant African snails that were destroying everyone's crops. But the wolfsnails then ate many other species of snails into extinction . . . and the giant African snails are still there!

Florida rosy wolfsnail

Jellyfish

The most spectacular gastropods are the 3,000 species of ocean-living nudibranchs (sometimes called *sea slugs*), and scientists think they may all be carnivorous! The **BLUE GLAUCUS** feeds on venomous jellies floating in the ocean, the **SPANISH SHAWL** eats anemones, while **FAVORINUS SEA SLUGS** eat *other* sea slugs!

Blue glaucus

Spanish shawl

Favorinus sea slug

Most slugs and snails are quite partial to lettuce, but from sucking down earthworms in Wales to eating species to extinction on Pacific islands, these slow-moving predators of the undergrowth are a reminder that even the animals we *think* we know really well can still surprise us.

ALL MINIBEASTS ARE TINY

WRONG!

Let's get one thing straight . . . some minibeasts are actually *smaller* than tiny. They are absolutely *miniscule*! If you grabbed a handful of soil, you would be holding thousands of them.

Fairy flies (which are really a type of wasp) like *KIKIKI HUNA* are microscopic – and smaller than some plants and animals that are made from a single cell. These wasps are so small they use their wispy wings like paddles because, at their size, air behaves more like a liquid than a gas.

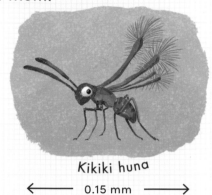
Kikiki huna
← 0.15 mm →

But on the other end of the scale, the tropics are *full* of mega-sized insects. Chinese *PHRYGANISTRIA STICK INSECTS* are the longest, with one species measuring an enormous 64 centimetres – that's longer than the average cat!

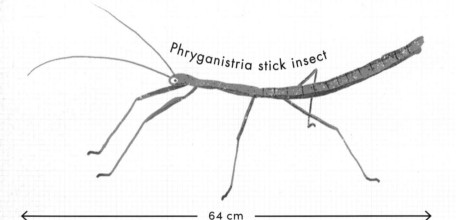
Phryganistria stick insect
← 64 cm →

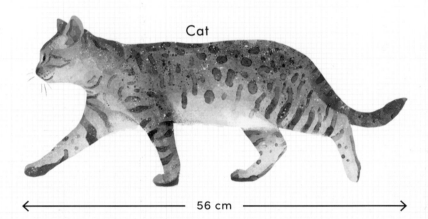
Cat
← 56 cm →

Giant grasshopper
← 24 cm →

Sparrow
← 21 cm →

If we're talking about wingspan, the *GIANT GRASSHOPPER* is excellently named. Its outstretched wings that carry it through the forests of Central and South America really are giant, reaching out wider than those of sparrows' and blue tits'.

The true heavyweights of the insect world are the *GOLIATH BEETLES* of tropical Africa. The winged adults can weigh up to 60 grams and their larvae can weigh up to a whopping 100 grams! The chunky *GIANT WETA* from New Zealand can reach this weight too . . . that's heavier than a common toad.

Common toad
40 g

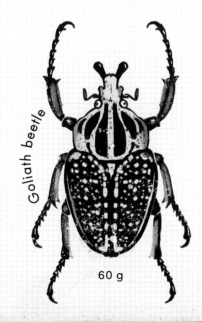
Goliath beetle
60 g

Some insects have evolved a truly incredible way to be big, but you might need to wrap your head around it . . .

Rather than *individually* growing larger in size, some 'social' insects, such as ants and termites, live together in enormous colonies, where individuals perform different jobs – some are workers, some are guards, some lay eggs and some find food. None of these termites or ants could survive on their own, just like one of your eyes or your liver not being able to survive without the rest of your body. But, by working together in these huge masses, scientists think these colonies of individual small insects actually work just like one single huge body – a superorganism.

Although colonies of termites might seem large with their hundreds of thousands of individuals, *LEAFCUTTER ANTS* are by far the largest type of superorganism, with some colonies in the American tropics containing millions of ants and stretching over 500 square metres.

Leafcutter ant

So although insects today physically can't grow much larger than a medium-sized bird, some have evolved an incredible way of working together as if they are one animal – reaching mind-bogglingly enormous sizes.

31

ALL 'WORMS' ARE WORMS

Loads of minibeasts that look like others are actually totally different kinds of living things. Take worms for example . . . or wormy-*looking* things. Some animals called worms aren't *really* the same kind of 'worms' as earthworms. Confused? Don't be!

Earthworm

Leech

Antarctic scale worm

Tapeworm

Feather duster worm

Pseudobiceros

Ribbon worm

Nematodes

EARTHWORMS are annelids – a massive group of almost 19,000 species, that include blood-sucking **LEECHES** and marine **FIREWORMS**. Most of them live in the oceans, like the giant deep-sea **ANTARCTIC SCALE WORM** or the beautiful **FEATHER DUSTER WORMS** that capture microscopic snacks with their feathery fans.

FLUKES, *TAPEWORMS* and *FLATWORMS* look wormy, but are all from another group of animals called the platyhelminths, and they aren't segmented like annelids are. Flukes and tapeworms all live inside other animals as parasites, feeding off their energy, but lots of flatworms live and move freely in wet places, like the sensational *PSEUDOBICEROS*.

RIBBON WORMS usually live in burrows in the sea floor. To catch their prey, some shoot a sticky, venomous net of tubes from their heads that works a bit like a dangerous glove being blown inside out.

The biggest group of 'worms' are the *NEMATODES*. There are possibly over a million species of these tiny animals living on everything, everywhere, in the soil, inside insects, on buildings, at the bottom of the ocean . . . They are incredibly important because they eat and clear away lots of mess like dried leaves and dead animals that would otherwise clutter the Earth.

Being thin and wriggly is a good look in the animal kingdom. That's because being thin and narrow at both ends means you can easily squeeze yourself into small gaps in search of a nice home or a tasty treat. And having a tube-like body means there isn't so much to go wrong with it! There are even more smaller groups of 'worms' that aren't really worms at all . . .

See-through ocean-living **ARROW WORMS** have quite scary-looking sharp teeth on their heads, which they pop out from under a protective hood when they're needed to snatch food.

Arrow worm

VELVET WORMS, with their stubby legs, look a little bit more like caterpillars, but those legs have claws on their ends. Velvet worms live on land and trap their prey by shooting jets of slime.

Velvet worm

HAIR WORMS spend their entire lives inside arthropods. They are incredibly long and thin (which is why they are named after hairs).

HORSESHOE WORMS are pretty animals that filter-feed on the sea floor. They have long bodies buried in the seabed, with only the very tips of them poking out into the water where they wave their colourful hairs to capture food, in a similar way to feather duster worms.

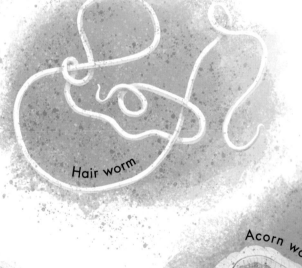
Hair worm

Acorn worm

Horseshoe worm

Finally, **ACORN WORMS** might look like any of these other long-bodied animals, but they are actually much, much, much more closely related to frogs, birds and *humans* than to any of the minibeasts in this entire book.

Remember, the next time you see something that looks a little bit wormy – especially if you're near the sea – it might not really be a *real* worm at all!

INSECTS ARE QUIET

WRONG!

If you were asked, "Which animals are loud?", you might think of a roaring lion, a deafening bellbird or, if you're *really* clever, a singing humpback whale, but insects aren't generally thought of as being very noisy.

Most insects rely on their incredible eyes to track movement (one type of butterfly even has eyes on its bottom!) and their sense of smell to track down food. They don't usually need their hearing to find their way, but for some the world is a very noisy place indeed . . .

GRASSHOPPERS and *WATER BOATMEN*, like many other insects that make loud chirping noises, rub bumpy parts of their body together like running a fingernail down a comb. This is called 'stridulation' and some insects, like some species of cricket, have hollow body parts to help make the sound larger – like the hollow inside of a guitar which makes the strings sound louder. Other insects, such as the *GIANT FIJIAN LONG-HORNED BEETLE*, make a loud hissing sound by forcing air out of their bodies.

Grasshopper

Water boatman

But often the smaller you are, the trickier it is to make a big noise . . . *DEATHWATCH BEETLES* aren't very large, so they hit their heads against rotting wood, which vibrates and makes a noise much larger than if the insect tried to make a sound themselves.

Giant Fijian long-horned beetle

Deathwatch beetle

The underground *MOLE CRICKET* does something just as smart, building chambers in their burrows to amplify their song, just like putting a speaker inside a bowl to increase the volume.

If making noise is important, then being an expert listener is too, and many insects have evolved ears that are super-sensitive to predators and other members of their species. *KATYDID CRICKETS* have ears on their legs just below their knees, while *LACEWINGS* have ears on their wings! *MOSQUITOES* listen using their antennae and *MANTIDS* even have a kind of ear in the middle of their chest.

Mosquito

Lacewing

Katydid cricket

Mantid

Tiger moth

Mole cricket

Having a brilliant sense of hearing is hugely important for the *TIGER MOTH* too. Not only have they evolved ears to listen out for their biggest enemy – the big brown bat – but when they hear one, they make very high-pitched clicks and squeaks. As the bat uses sonar to 'see' its prey through sound, it gets completely confused and ends up missing a tasty moth snack.

So while we might think of insects living in a quieter world than the one we know, it can also get pretty rowdy too.

IF IT HAS EIGHT LEGS . . . IT'S A SPIDER WRONG!

If you see something scuttling around your bathroom and you count eight legs rather than six, then it'll be a type of minibeast called an arachnid, and most likely a spider – half all arachnid species are . . . That's about 45,000 that we know about! However, there are a whole bunch of other arachnids that have eight legs but definitely *aren't* spiders . . .

Red bark scorpion

SCORPIONS are the most well-known non-spider arachnids. These venomous predators can live in very dry conditions where they use their pincers and stings to ambush their prey.

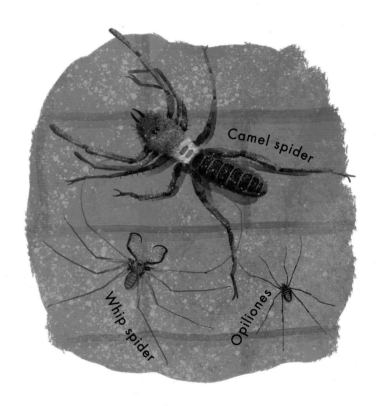

Camel spider

Whip spider

Opiliones

Unlike spiders, 'harvestmen' (the *OPILIONES*) have minute bodies that are fused together into just one section, often with a small platform on top for their eyes to look around from.

WHIP SPIDERS can't make silk like spiders and don't use venom despite their fearsome appearance. Like *CAMEL SPIDERS* (which also aren't *really* spiders!) they actually only use three pairs of legs for walking. Their front two 'legs' are used to feel their way around. They also have extra spiny arachnid limbs specially for grabbing prey and feeding.

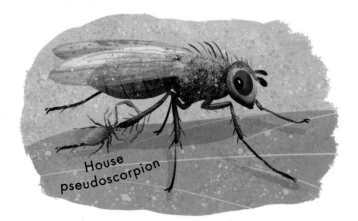

House pseudoscorpion

PSEUDOSCORPIONS are *tiny* arachnids that look a little like their larger namesakes. Some species, like the *HOUSE PSEUDOSCORPION*, hunt other arachnids after hitching rides on flies' undercarriages as they fly into people's homes.

Demodex

Finally, the ticks and mites (known as acari) are usually *almost* too small to be spotted easily, but they live everywhere from inside dusty books to on our pets' skin. In fact, our *faces* are home to two species of *DEMODEX* mites that live face down in the pores of our hairs!

MINI FACT!

There is another type of minibeast that has eight legs which isn't a spider or an arachnid. In fact, they're not even arthropods . . . *TARDIGRADES* are adorable microscopic animals that clamber over moss and lichen on their eight chunky legs, hoovering up plant cells, bacteria and other smaller tardigrades.

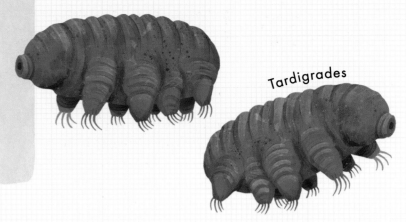

Tardigrades

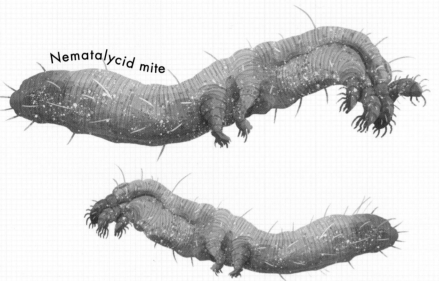

Nematalycid mite

Although eight long legs is the usual for arachnids, there are some species that make do with fewer (or less impressive) feet.

NEMATALYCID MITES, for instance, are so small that they live in between grains of sand. In order to slip easily into these microscopic spaces, their legs have become very short and their body has elongated into a more worm-like shape. This reduction in the size of legs is found in many sorts of animals that live underground, from legless reptiles to stubby-armed mammals.

However, *some* other tiny mites, like rust mites, have actually *completely* lost some of their legs and only have two pairs left. And some female *PODAPOLIPID* mites, which live on insects, lose their legs altogether as adults (although others, like *EATONIANA PLUMIPES*, have evolved very fancy hindlimbs indeed!).

Although animals are usually built following a recognisable plan, evolution often creates species that seem to bend the rules of what grown-ups say animals "should look like".

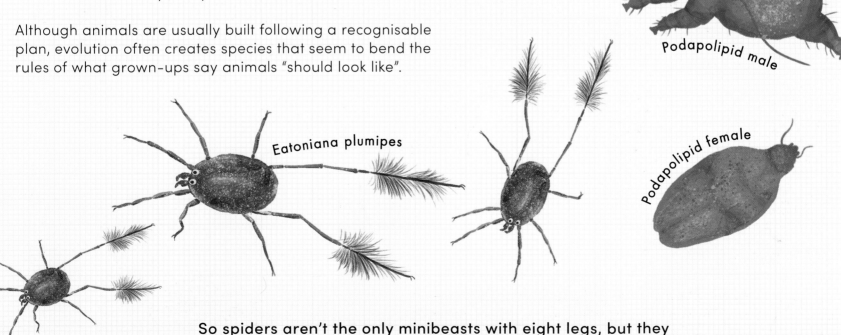

Podapolipid male

Eatoniana plumipes

Podapolipid female

So spiders aren't the only minibeasts with eight legs, but they are the most likely arachnid you'll see in your bathroom . . .

ALL SPIDERS CATCH PREY IN WEBS

Spider webs are incredible traps for catching flies, moths and other animals. The super-strong silk is covered in a sticky glue-like substance that holds unlucky victims fast and actually sucks flying insects on to them through the build-up of static electricity! But not all spiders catch their prey by building a web in the air . . .

Goldenrod crab spider

Some crab spiders, such as the *GOLDENROD CRAB SPIDER*, are expertly camouflaged ambush predators that sit and wait for prey where they are likely to appear (like in the centre of a nectar-filled flower).

Other spiders, such the *LYNX SPIDER*, also strike at prey visiting plants. Their eight eyes are arranged in a circle on the top of their head so they can spot any approaching visitors.

Lynx spider

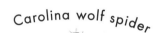

Carolina wolf spider

Wolf spiders, like the 3-centimetre-long *CAROLINA WOLF SPIDER*, do not wait for prey to come to them but actively hunt insects, searching for food.

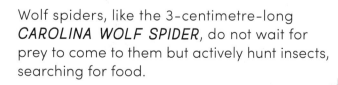

Blue-faced jumping spider

The 5,000 species of jumping spiders, like the *BLUE-FACED JUMPING SPIDER*, are also solitary predators who rely, like wolf and lynx spiders, on excellent 3D vision in order to accurately lunge after their prey.

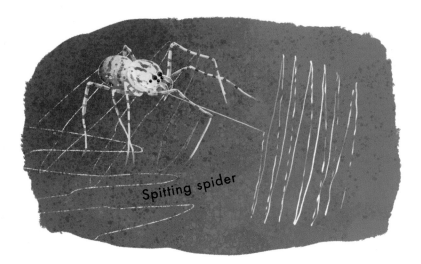

Spitting spider

Rather than using silk from their back ends to build webs, *SPITTING SPIDERS* spew a high-speed sticky zigzag of gooey silk from their mouthparts to imprison prey in a deadly cage.

Myrmekiaphila neilyoungi

Trapdoor spiders, like **MYRMEKIAPHILA NEILYOUNGI** (named after the Canadian musician Neil Young), hide in silk-lined tunnels sealed off by a trapdoor held in place by a silk hinge. When they sense the vibrations of prey walking nearby, they pounce out to ambush their unsuspecting victim.

Antilles pinktoe tarantula

Lastly, although some of the 1,000 species of tarantula, like the **ANTILLES PINKTOE TARANTULA**, *do* spin funnel webs — these are to live in, like a self-made hammock. They hunt by ambushing arthropods, piercing their armour with their large hard fangs, as well other small animals like rodents and birds.

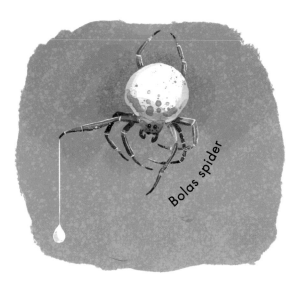

Bolas spider

BOLAS SPIDERS catch moths, but not in webs. Instead, they swing and fling sticky globules on the end of silk ropes at them to snatch them from mid-air.

Diving bell spider

Of the spiders that do spin webs, not all of them are used for trapping prey. The *DIVING BELL SPIDER* uses its web to trap air to breathe underwater, like a scuba diver's tank, so it can live almost entirely underwater.

Most people think that if an animal is a spider, it spins a web, but only about half of the 45,000 species of spiders catch prey by doing this. Although all spiders have silk in common, the amazing ability to spin webs is only one way to catch a snack.

FALSE WIDOW SPIDERS AND DADDY-LONG-LEGS ARE DEADLY VENOMOUS

WRONG!

Some people say that daddy-long-legs are so venomous they could kill a human . . . if only they were able to pierce people's skin, even though it's totally WRONG!

It *is* actually possible for daddy-long-legs spiders to pierce human skin, but it would only make a microscopic hole because their fangs are less than half a millimetre long. And their venom? Well, for mammals, it's so weak it's like it doesn't even exist.

FALSE WIDOW SPIDERS can cause mayhem, with humans sometimes closing down schools if one is spotted! They look a *little* bit like the famous *BLACK WIDOW SPIDER* from Australia (which *is* very venomous), but the *false* widow spiders? Not so much! If you annoyed one, you might get a little nip that might feel like a bee sting . . . but that's it.

Black widow spider

False widow spider

Daddy-long-legs

Scary-sounding names can turn people against insects too. Spare a thought for the 'murder hornet', which doesn't sound so bad when called its other name, the *ASIAN GIANT HORNET.* They are very large wasps and, yes, they can sting through beekeepers' suits, but when treated with the same respect as any other species of wasp, they are actually much less risky than some of their other yellow-and-black cousins.

Asian giant hornet

MINI FACT!

The name 'daddy-long-legs' is used by different people to talk about three completely different types of minibeast – the spider, crane flies and harvestmen. But they are all completely harmless to humans.

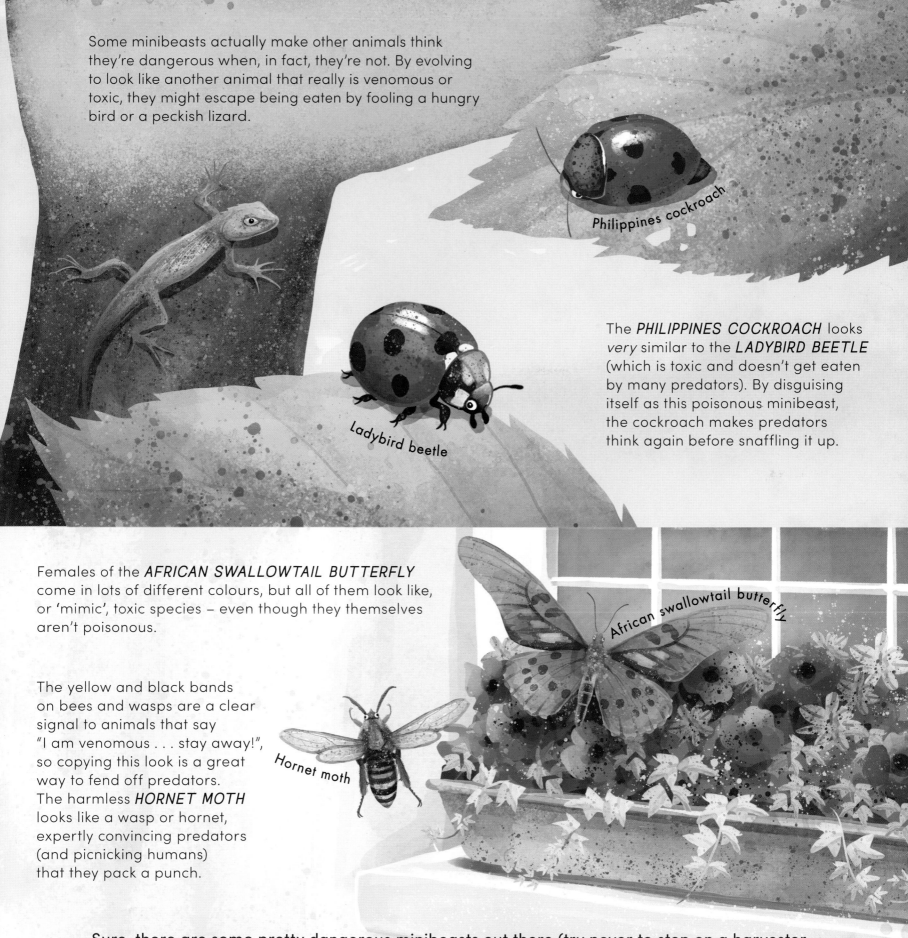

Some minibeasts actually make other animals think they're dangerous when, in fact, they're not. By evolving to look like another animal that really is venomous or toxic, they might escape being eaten by fooling a hungry bird or a peckish lizard.

Philippines cockroach

Ladybird beetle

The *PHILIPPINES COCKROACH* looks *very* similar to the *LADYBIRD BEETLE* (which is toxic and doesn't get eaten by many predators). By disguising itself as this poisonous minibeast, the cockroach makes predators think again before snaffling it up.

Females of the *AFRICAN SWALLOWTAIL BUTTERFLY* come in lots of different colours, but all of them look like, or 'mimic', toxic species – even though they themselves aren't poisonous.

The yellow and black bands on bees and wasps are a clear signal to animals that say "I am venomous . . . stay away!", so copying this look is a great way to fend off predators. The harmless *HORNET MOTH* looks like a wasp or hornet, expertly convincing predators (and picnicking humans) that they pack a punch.

Hornet moth

African swallowtail butterfly

Sure, there are some pretty dangerous minibeasts out there (try never to step on a harvester ant or brush against a saddleback caterpillar if you live in North America!), but try not to go over the top with your fear. Only a tiny, *tiny* number of arthropods are in any way dangerous, and minibeasts would much rather avoid going anywhere near a giant human than defend themselves at close quarters from a curious set of fingers.

COCKROACHES ARE INDESTRUCTIBLE

WRONG!

There are over 4,500 species of cockroaches, but most people just think about the ones that hang around where humans live (and sometimes eat!). Because cockroaches can thrive in huge numbers in places other animals would find it hard to live in, people often say that they're so tough they could live forever.

They're not *indestructible*, but cockroaches ARE tough. Some can survive without eating for a whole month, they can swim if caught in a flood, and the *JAPANESE COCKROACH* can even survive sub-zero temperatures when it's young.

But the reason behind their success has less to do with their toughness, and a lot to do with how they breed.

Cockroaches lay *lots* of eggs *very* quickly, so if only a few cockroaches survive after a fire or a building being destroyed, they can be found in massive numbers soon afterwards. It's this super-fast way they reproduce that helps them recover after any sort of disaster, which can fool people into thinking that they can survive anything.

Cockroaches may be pretty tough but they can't survive everything. In fact, there are some things happening on Earth that insects would be very worried about if they could understand what was going on.

The truth is, more than 40% of insect species are becoming rarer each year and a third are classified as 'endangered'. This is happening all over the world – from butterflies being lost in the UK countryside to species of bumblebees disappearing forever in parts of the USA. The reason for this is what we humans are doing to the Earth.

As humans have built on top of land all around the world, they have cut down and paved over lots of environments where insects have evolved to hunt for food, find mates, and build their homes.

Many of these environments have been changed into farmland where only a few types of plants are grown. The fewer sorts of plants that are found in a place, the fewer number of insects that can exist there. Some pesticides used to protect the plants grown for human food and fuel from insects that like to eat them can kill lots more insects than they need to.

The changing climate is also a big problem for some insects, as unusual weather patterns means some species are emerging at different times of the year to the species they hunt, so they find less food.

Insects have survived five mass extinctions throughout the history of life on Earth, but today they're in trouble because of changes that one species, humans, have made to the natural world. But people can change their ways! By protecting insects' homes, letting more wild flowers and plants grow on farms and slowing climate change, we can make sure the minibeasts in this book are still around for years to come.

We can all play a part in helping insects to survive, and while no insect is truly indestructible, the *DIABOLICAL IRONCLAD BEETLE* comes pretty close. Thanks to a fused pair of super-strong wing casings, this beetle can withstand not only being trodden on, but even driven over by a car!

INSECTS ONLY LIVE IN WARM PLACES  WRONG!

Out of all the millions of species without backbones that have evolved on Planet Earth over the past 3.5 billion years, only some species have become truly land-based, while most crustaceans and other invertebrates are still mostly connected to water.

Although they live in almost every habitat on Earth, insects are cold-blooded and are usually limited to warm places or warmer times of year. But there are some adventurous species that can be found in extremely tricky places to make a living . . .

Bombus polaris

Isabella tiger moth caterpillar

Brown-and-black woolly bear caterpillars are the larvae of the *ISABELLA TIGER MOTH* and can be found within the Arctic Circle. Not only do the caterpillars live in incredibly cold conditions, they hatch just before the winter and then freeze solid, only thawing out when the weather warms the following year.

Isabella tiger moth

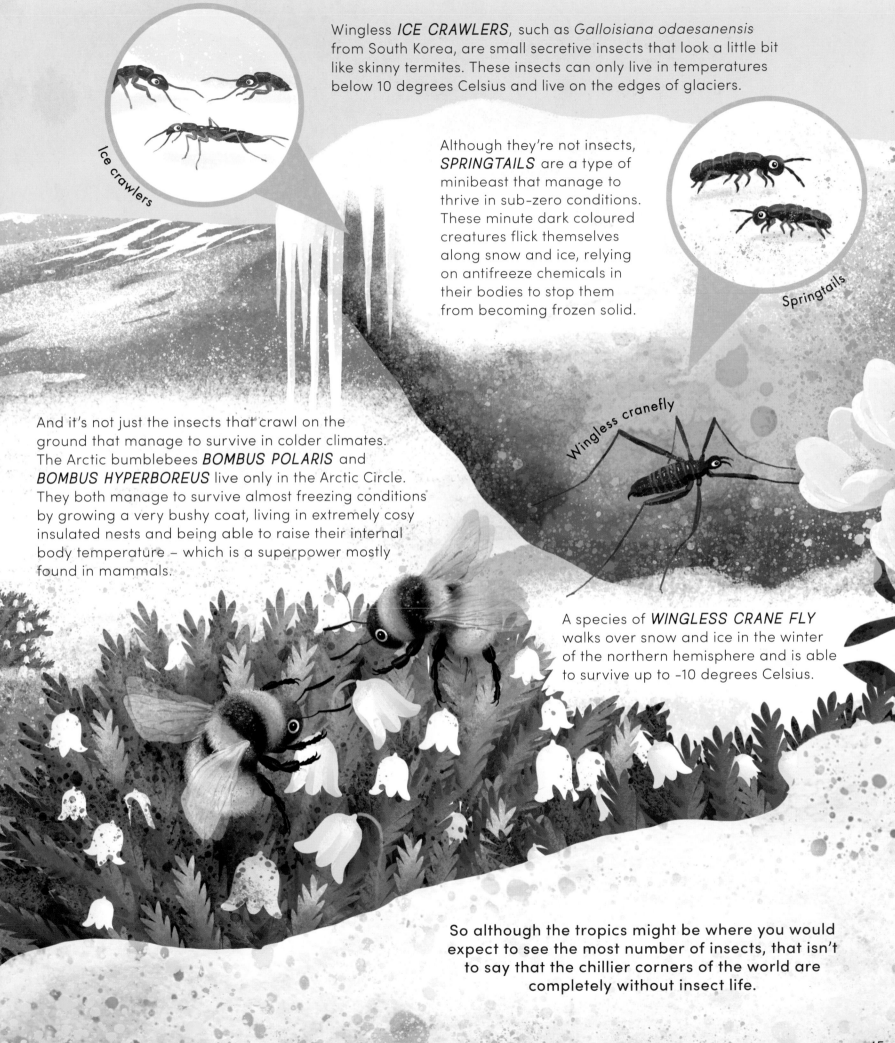

Wingless *ICE CRAWLERS*, such as *Galloisiana odaesanensis* from South Korea, are small secretive insects that look a little bit like skinny termites. These insects can only live in temperatures below 10 degrees Celsius and live on the edges of glaciers.

Ice crawlers

Although they're not insects, *SPRINGTAILS* are a type of minibeast that manage to thrive in sub-zero conditions. These minute dark coloured creatures flick themselves along snow and ice, relying on antifreeze chemicals in their bodies to stop them from becoming frozen solid.

Springtails

Wingless cranefly

And it's not just the insects that crawl on the ground that manage to survive in colder climates. The Arctic bumblebees *BOMBUS POLARIS* and *BOMBUS HYPERBOREUS* live only in the Arctic Circle. They both manage to survive almost freezing conditions by growing a very bushy coat, living in extremely cosy insulated nests and being able to raise their internal body temperature – which is a superpower mostly found in mammals.

A species of *WINGLESS CRANE FLY* walks over snow and ice in the winter of the northern hemisphere and is able to survive up to -10 degrees Celsius.

So although the tropics might be where you would expect to see the most number of insects, that isn't to say that the chillier corners of the world are completely without insect life.

CRUSTACEANS ONLY LIVE IN WATER

WRONG!

Crustaceans are insects' aquatic cousins. These watery arthropods are found throughout the world's oceans and rivers and are super-diverse in their shapes and behaviours, from the microscopic copepods to giant isopods, and even parasitic whale 'lice' that cling to mammal giants.

But although crustaceans are thought of as the insects of the sea, 3% of the 50,000 species of crustaceans now call the land their home . . .

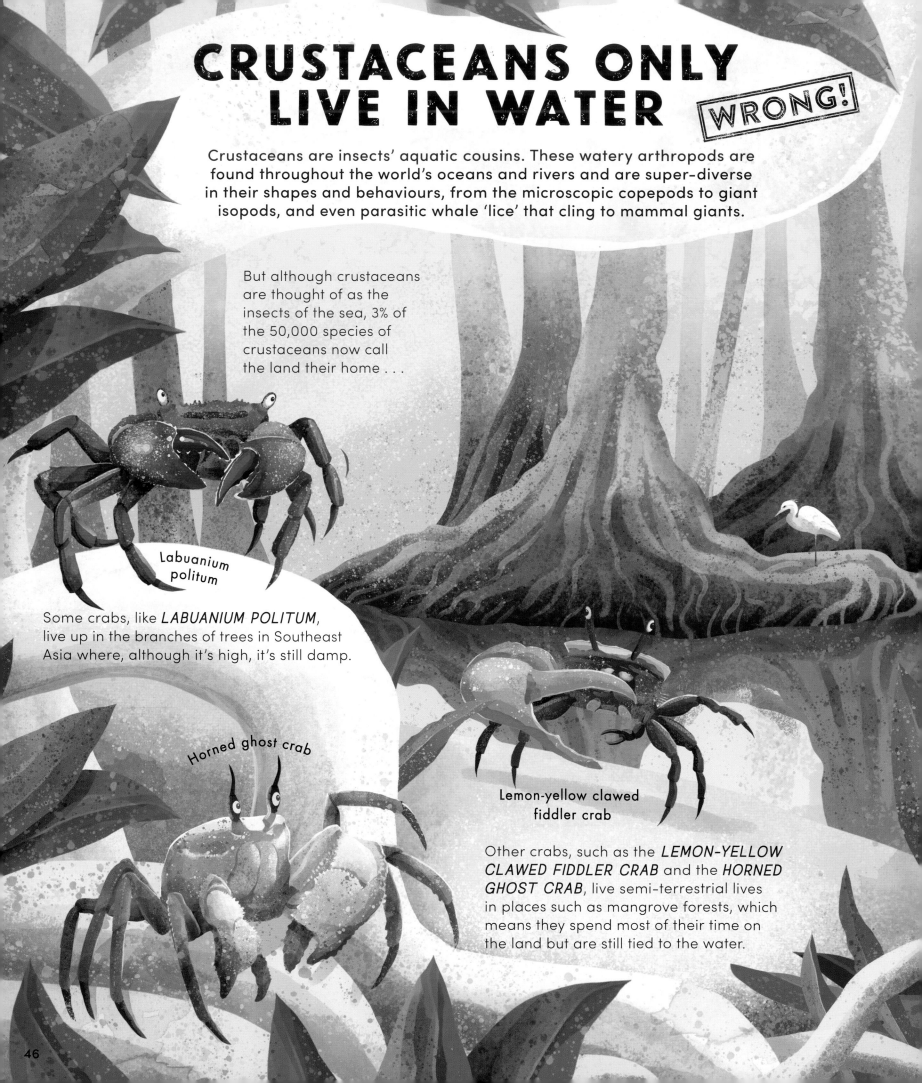

Labuanium politum

Some crabs, like *LABUANIUM POLITUM*, live up in the branches of trees in Southeast Asia where, although it's high, it's still damp.

Horned ghost crab

Lemon-yellow clawed fiddler crab

Other crabs, such as the *LEMON-YELLOW CLAWED FIDDLER CRAB* and the *HORNED GHOST CRAB*, live semi-terrestrial lives in places such as mangrove forests, which means they spend most of their time on the land but are still tied to the water.

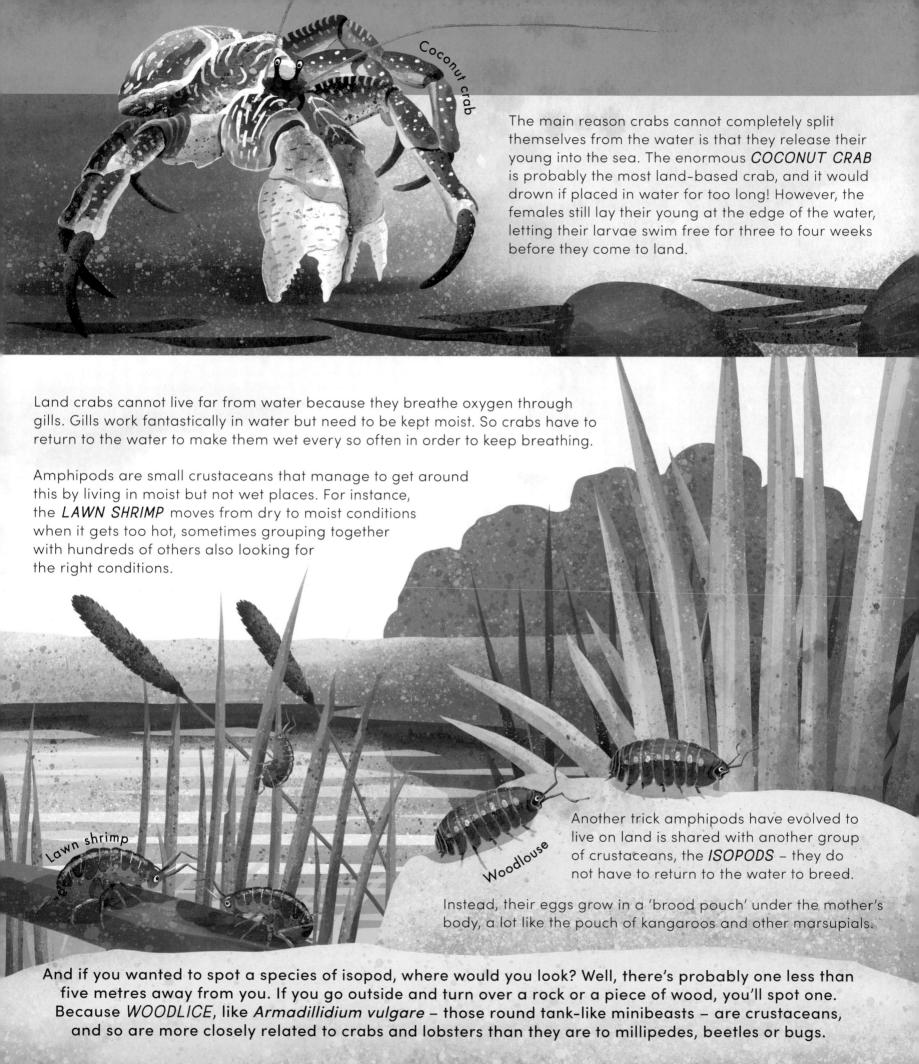

The main reason crabs cannot completely split themselves from the water is that they release their young into the sea. The enormous *COCONUT CRAB* is probably the most land-based crab, and it would drown if placed in water for too long! However, the females still lay their young at the edge of the water, letting their larvae swim free for three to four weeks before they come to land.

Land crabs cannot live far from water because they breathe oxygen through gills. Gills work fantastically in water but need to be kept moist. So crabs have to return to the water to make them wet every so often in order to keep breathing.

Amphipods are small crustaceans that manage to get around this by living in moist but not wet places. For instance, the *LAWN SHRIMP* moves from dry to moist conditions when it gets too hot, sometimes grouping together with hundreds of others also looking for the right conditions.

Another trick amphipods have evolved to live on land is shared with another group of crustaceans, the *ISOPODS* – they do not have to return to the water to breed.

Instead, their eggs grow in a 'brood pouch' under the mother's body, a lot like the pouch of kangaroos and other marsupials.

And if you wanted to spot a species of isopod, where would you look? Well, there's probably one less than five metres away from you. If you go outside and turn over a rock or a piece of wood, you'll spot one. Because *WOODLICE*, like *Armadillidium vulgare* – those round tank-like minibeasts – are crustaceans, and so are more closely related to crabs and lobsters than they are to millipedes, beetles or bugs.

BUTTERFLIES EMERGE FROM COCOONS

WRONG!

When you were very little, you might have had famous stories read to you about butterflies emerging from cocoons. Now, let's just get this out of the way . . . Butterflies. Don't. Emerge. From. Cocoons!

Cocoons are protective casings that *MOTHS* build around themselves when they transform into their pupa stage; it's like an extra layer of protection. Moths build their cocoons out of silk, but others, like *BAGWORMS*, also include small sticks, soil and leaves.

Butterflies never build woven cocoons. Instead, when they transform into a butterfly, caterpillars depend on camouflage or warning colours to protect them while they're in their pupa (or soft chrysalis) phase.

Bagworm

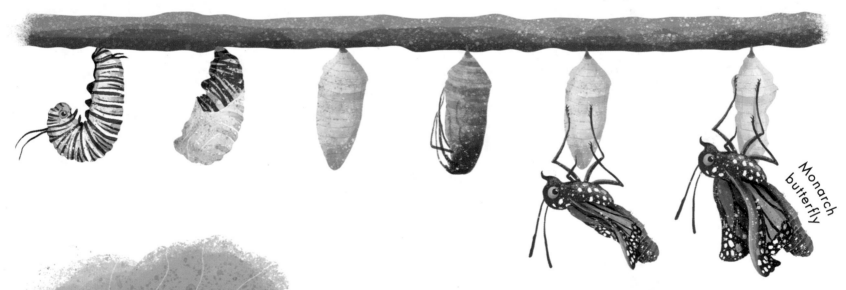

Monarch butterfly

Ladybird larvae

Now, let's get on to the interesting stuff . . . The first incredible way of becoming an adult is called *HOLOMETABOLOUS METAMORPHOSIS* (which means 'complete' change) and it's how over 80% of insects grow up. Butterflies, beetles, ants and flies all begin life as larvae – these are usually sausage-shaped eating machines and very different-looking creatures to how they will look at the end of their lives (although many, like *LADYBIRD BEETLE LARVAE*, can look spectacular).

This transformation is ingenious because it means the insect can do two very different things extremely well by using two types of body. First, in its larval form, it can dedicate its life to eating and growing, while, as an adult, it becomes a first-class flying machine – and expert in travelling and making babies.

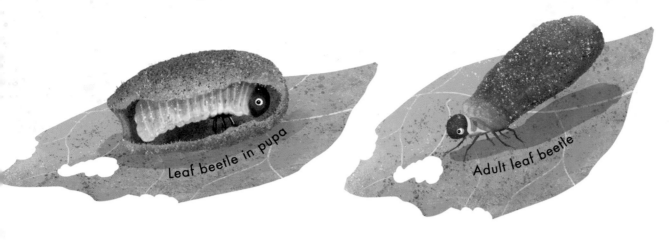

Leaf beetle in pupa

Adult leaf beetle

Right! Now we've got that sorted, let's take a look at the rest of the insects to discover that emerging from a pupa (or, as in some *LEAF BEETLES*, a chamber made from your own poo) isn't the only way to grow up.

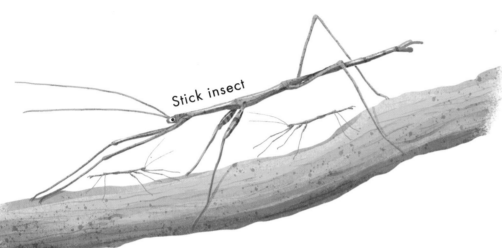

Stick insect

HEMIMETABOLOUS METAMORPHOSIS (which means 'gradual' change), is not as common as complete change, but it's what happens to *GRASSHOPPERS*, *STICK INSECTS*, *DRAGONFLIES* and *BUGS*. Rather than spending time as larvae they emerge from eggs as tiny (usually cute) versions of their adult forms. During this stage they are called 'nymphs' and, as they grow and shed their exoskeleton, they turn into slightly larger versions of themselves.

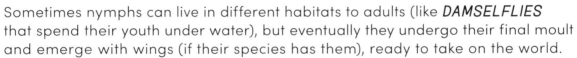

Sometimes nymphs can live in different habitats to adults (like *DAMSELFLIES* that spend their youth under water), but eventually they undergo their final moult and emerge with wings (if their species has them), ready to take on the world.

Damselfly nymph

Damselfly

Finally, a third, rare way of growing up is *AMETABOLOUS GROWTH*, where the insect undergoes only a tiny amount of change in body shape from young to adult . . . They just get bigger! This is how wingless *SILVERFISH* grow – even though they may go through 60 moults during their life, their body hardly changes at all.

Silverfish

So next time you overhear someone explaining that hungry caterpillars emerge as butterflies from cocoons . . . you know what to tell them!

BUTTERFLIES AREN'T VERY POWERFUL

WRONG!

Butterflies have a wimpy reputation: they flutter about on tissue-thin wings, tossed around by the wind, trying to avoid being eaten by all sorts of other animals as they go about their day. But many of these lightweight vegetarians are actually pretty hardcore!

Lots of butterflies pack a mighty wallop: they're poisonous! One way to become poisonous is to eat toxic foods and then keep the toxins for yourself. That's just what *MONARCH BUTTERFLIES* do, by feeding on toxic milkweed plants and storing the poison in their bodies.

Monarch

Goliath birdwing

The *GOLIATH BIRDWING* from Indonesia is toxic too, and lets its enemies know this by being brightly coloured yellow-green against black – which is animal code for, "Don't eat me or you'll be sorry!".

Painted lady

Non-poisonous butterflies are often high-speed champions – some of the fastest butterflies are *SKIPPERS*, which can fly at an impressive 45 kilometres per hour or faster – so they're not just being blown around on the wind.

Skipper

Other butterflies, despite their fragile appearance, manage to survive incredible journeys. *PAINTED LADY BUTTERFLIES* travel thousands of miles on epic migrations, from North Africa and central Asia to the Arctic Circle. It takes the butterflies about six generations to complete this 14,500-kilometre relay race, flying over 500 metres above the surface of the Earth.

It's not just full-grown butterflies that are secretly powerful. Some caterpillar defences are extreme! And even more so in the butterflies' cousins, the moths.

Many caterpillars might look cute and fluffy, but that fluff is really made of hundreds of toxic stinging hairs. Just a brush against the *HICKORY TUSSOCK CATERPILLAR*'s fur can bring humans out in a very nasty rash.

Hickory tussock caterpillar

Puss caterpillar

The spectacular *PUSS CATERPILLAR* is even more toxic. Venomous spines hidden within the hairy fluff-ball can result in pain shooting all the way up a human's arm, vomiting and a very, very upset stomach.

Theroa zethus

Orchard butterfly caterpillar

Some caterpillars use shock tactics to warn off predators. The *ORCHARD BUTTERFLY* disguises itself as a bird dropping but, if an animal works out it might be a tasty snack, it shoots out a pair of bright red smelly 'horns' to scare the attacker away.

Some moth caterpillars, like those of *THEROA ZETHUS*, shoot something even worse out – a fine spray of acid to keep predators at bay.

Orchard butterfly

From long-distance champions to acid-spraying caterpillars, butterflies (and moths) are a little more mighty than they usually get credit for.

ALL INSECTS LAY EGGS

WRONG!

OK! You might have seen insect eggs stuck to the side of a plant stem or in a snug hole in a wall, and that's because most insects lay eggs. But there are, as you might expect by now . . .
EXCEPTIONS TO THE RULE!

Let's start with *where* some eggs hatch, as not all species lay their eggs on the safe, shady underside of a leaf. For instance, a group of insects called parasitoids, such as *CONCURA WASPS*, are insects that lay their eggs *inside* other insects. After injecting their eggs into an unfortunate host through their long tube-like ovipositor, their larvae hatch and eat the host from the inside-out!

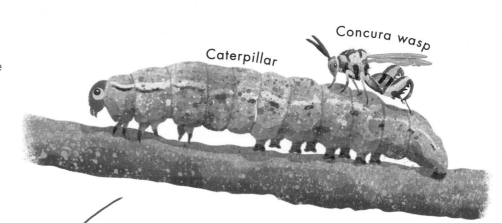

Caterpillar

Concura wasp

Pacific beetle cockroach

Other insects, like the *PACIFIC BEETLE COCKROACH*, don't lay eggs at all. Instead, they let their eggs hatch *inside them*, and then 'give birth' to live young, after feeding them on a milky substance to help them grow.

Some species of *FLIES* also hatch their young inside themselves. When they finally 'give birth', their young are already wrapped in a hard skin called a puparium and are able to survive until they emerge as adult flies the next year.

Tsetse fly

Some female insects, like the *YELLOW UMBRELLA STICK INSECT* from Indonesia, don't need to find a mate but can just produce identical clones of themselves.

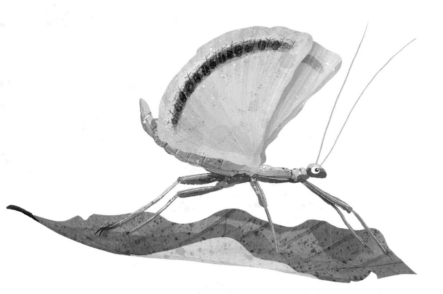

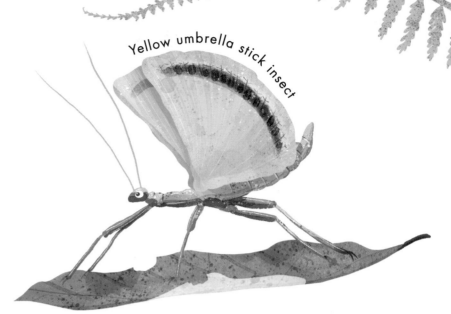

Yellow umbrella stick insect

Amazingly, the *APHIDS* you might find in your garden also do this and produce their clones as live births. Even more amazingly, those baby aphids already have baby clones of themselves inside them ready to be born later.

Aphid

Earwig

Finally, most people think of insects as being fairly simple creatures that might lay eggs and then forget about them. But some insects are actually fantastic parents. Female *EARWIGS* take extremely good care of their clutch of eggs by cleaning them, protecting them from predators and feeding them after they hatch.

As insects are such an incredibly enormous group of animals, it's impossible to find something they all do in exactly the same way. It's not surprising then that they have evolved such different ways of making sure their young survive. Nature finds a way!

HUMANS ARE BETTER BUILDERS THAN INSECTS

Humans have built some pretty tall buildings and a few epic bridges in the last 200 years or so, but insects have been building amazingly complicated structures for a lot longer than that . . .

TERMITES' mounds are built from chewed-up mud and poo, and the clever insides of the mounds mean the air within them never goes stale. They can last for 2,000 years, and if they were built on a human scale, they would be as tall as the tallest skyscraper on Earth.

Termites

Bees

BEES store eggs, young bees, pollen and honey in cells, that are made from wax. They squeeze wax out of their own bodies and, in order to use as little wax as possible, they build cells as six-sided hexagons so they can all cram close together with no wasted space.

Paper wasps

Like termites, *PAPER WASPS* also build things out of materials they have chewed. By munching up old wood and plant stems, these wasps make a strong but light paper-like material that they build their huge nests with.

Leafcutter ant

Building structures is impressive, but the underground homes of *LEAFCUTTER ANTS* are entire insect cities. They are built around 'fungus gardens', which are connected by 'roads' to rubbish tips, food halls and even police stations!

And some insects make structures out of their own bodies!

When hundreds of thousands of **ARMY ANTS** need to cross a gap or a hole, a few of them stretch across, holding on to one another, and build a living bridge to help their fellow ants. They never let the bridge get too heavy and can build four or five in a day.

Army ant

ARMY ANTS also set up camps so the queen can rest as they move territory. These 'bivouacs' are made up of the ants' own bodies and protect the queen along with their defenceless larvae.

FIRE ANTS have even found a way to save the queen from a watery doom by building boats out of themselves when water rises! By riding on the floating younger members of the group, most of the ants don't even touch the water, the queen stays cosy, snug and dry in the centre of the raft.

Fire ants

Humans are certainly clever when it comes to building things, but insects have been making air-conditioned skyscrapers and ships out of their own bodies for millions of years before we ever picked up a hammer. In fact, a lot of scientists study insects to try to make even better, smarter structures for humans.

STUDYING INSECTS IS EXPENSIVE

WRONG!

Science labs can be full of pricey machines, but while some scientists need to use atom-bashing particle accelerators or number-crunching supercomputers, entomologists can use a lot of tools that aren't very expensive at all.

Moths are drawn to bright lights at night-time, so if you shine a light on a big *HANGING SHEET*, you'll soon be surrounded by a whole host of fluttering friends to identify. It doesn't get much simpler than this!

A *POOTER* is made of two flexible tubes with a clear cylinder at the end. By sucking on one of these tubes, insects are whizzed into the cylinder where they can be looked at closely. One of the tubes has a thin material covering the end, so you don't end up with a dung beetle in your mouth!

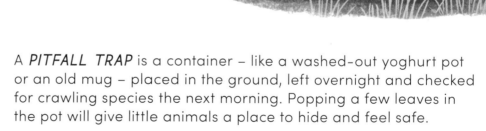

A *PITFALL TRAP* is a container – like a washed-out yoghurt pot or an old mug – placed in the ground, left overnight and checked for crawling species the next morning. Popping a few leaves in the pot will give little animals a place to hide and feel safe.

HAND LENSES are like pocket-sized microscopes and they are to entomologists what calculators are to mathematicians. A good entomologist is never without their trusty hand lens.

KICK NETS are fine-meshed nets used in fast-flowing water to check what aquatic invertebrates live in streams.

Sweeping backwards and forwards over long grass with a sturdy *SWEEP NET* is a great way to find insects living a few centimetres off the ground. Afterwards some entomologists turn the net inside out into a tray to see what species they might have captured, but others put their heads inside the net to have a look around.

A small *JAR OR POT* (or beaker or cup) is always important to have in your backpack in case you need to carry a specimen to a brighter spot for a closer look. Always try to release insects near to where you found them, though.

Computers and phones make taking notes easy, but on a drizzly day it's best to avoid electronics. Out in the field, a *WATERPROOF NOTEBOOK* and pencil are the best tools for making quick sketches about your discoveries.

When insects are brought back to the lab, entomologists can study them with fancy equipment like electron microscopes or X-ray scanners, but being a good scientist doesn't always rely on pricey gadgets. Sometimes a jar and a notebook are all you need to make great observations.

PEOPLE DON'T NEED INSECTS

Within their natural ecosystems, insects are astronomically important. They act as food for countless other species, recycle huge numbers of leaves and tons of fallen plant material, break up soil to help plants grow, and eat up poo and the remains of dead animals that would otherwise litter the floor.

Trichogramma wasp

But sometimes it's hard to imagine that humans actually need insects around – especially when your picnic's been invaded by a horsefly, or you can't find that mosquito in your bedroom at two o'clock in the morning . . .

On farms, insects are very important for protecting crops grown for humans to eat. Insects have been used since 300 BCE when Chinese farmers used ants to control pests that were damaging lemons. Today miniscule *TRICHOGRAMMA WASPS* help farmers to protect vegetables, cereals and cotton harvests from moths over 10 million hectares.

Other insects, like *DUNG BEETLES* in South America, also help keep cattle farms clean from massive build-ups of dung.

Dung beetle

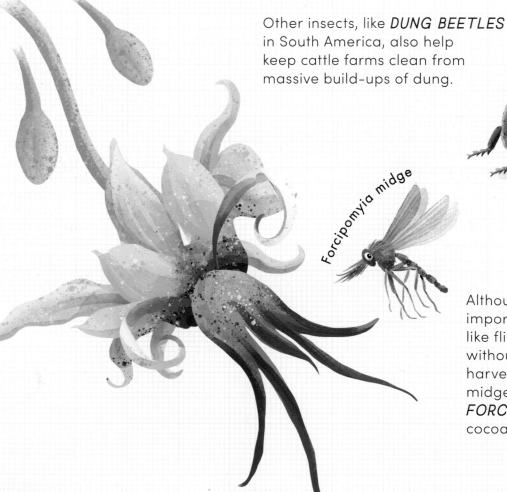

Forcipomyia midge

Although we usually think of bees as the most important pollinators, many other insect species like flies and moths also help plants to breed, and without them we wouldn't be able to grow and harvest some very important foods. If you think midges are just annoying, think again! We have *FORCIPOMYIA MIDGES* to thank for pollinating cocoa, without which we wouldn't have chocolate.

Diamphidia beetle larvae

Bombyx mori moth

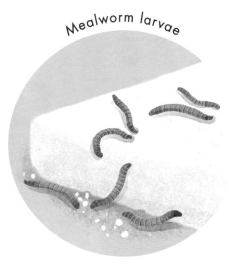

Mealworm larvae

Toxins from **DIAMPHIDIA BEETLE LARVAE** have been used by the indigenous people of the Kalahari in Africa for thousands of years to make their arrow darts for hunting exceptionally lethal.

If you are wearing anything made from silk, you have the larvae of the **BOMBYX MORI MOTH** to thank, which weaves the silk for their cocoons.

Insects might even hold the key to reducing the pollution people have littered the planet with, for example, **MEALWORM LARVAE** eat polystyrene.

Many ants, like the **FIRE ANT** and species of **LEAFCUTTER ANTS**, are being studied as they hold secrets to fighting infections, which might save many people's lives. Venom from certain species might actually be helpful rather than painful and it's being studied to try to find all kinds of new medicines.

Leafcutter ants

Sometimes it's hard to see that people are connected so closely with nature, especially if we live in a built-up urban place. But it's incredibly important that we look after the species we depend on so we don't lose everything we gain from them being around.

MINIBEASTS DON'T NEED US

WRONG!

If you've reached the end of this book, it means that you are now carrying around a whole *hive* of facts that you can use to DEFEND MINIBEASTS from the injustice of MISINFORMATION!

You see, a lot of people try to avoid minibeasts. They will never be as popular as fluffy mammals or scaly reptiles, and some people just think of minibeasts as 'creepy' crawlies (which is rather rude).

There's nothing *really* wrong with that. But when people avoid things, they tend to not want to learn more about them. And by not learning about them, they never unlearn false 'facts' like the ones we've overturned in this book! They just keep on thinking that they eat spiders in their sleep, that centipedes have 100 legs and that there's no point to insects.

Humans – by building things, spraying chemicals, destroying habitats and moving species around the world – have caused the number of minibeasts on Earth to shrink over the last 100 years, and a big reason why is that not very many people cared about them.

But you can only really care about something if you are interested in it. And the minibeasts of the world need our care. Let's make sure everyone is interested in – and then cares about – the little guys!

So the next time someone says something like "butterflies emerge from cocoons", why not tell them how interesting, surprising, numerous and incredible minibeasts really are?!

INDEX